CHERISHED MEMORIES

To my
favorite
Prayer
Warriors

Kelly
Simpson

Kelly Simpson
Cherished Memories

Published by BooxAi

ISBN: 978-965-577-945-5

Cherished Memories

My Story, No Shame, No Blame!

Kelly Simpson

Contents

PREFACE

IN THE BOOK The velveteen rabbit,

The Skin Horse tells the rabbit that being "Real isn't how you are made" "It's a thing that happens to you. When a child loves you for a long, long time, not just to play with, but REALLY loves you, then you become Real! The rabbit asks, "Does it hurt?" "Sometimes" said the Skin Horse, for he was always truthful. "When you are Real, you don't mind being hurt" The rabbit asks "Does it happen all at once, like being wound up?" "Or bit by bit" To which The Skin Horse replied "It doesn't happen all at once" "You become. It takes a long time. That's why it doesn't happen to people who break easily, or have sharp edges, or who must be carefully kept. Generally, by the time you are Real, most of your hair has been loved off, and your eyes drop out and you get loose in the joints and very shabby. But these things don't matter at all, because once you are Real, you can't be ugly, except to people who don't understand."

If you have never read the book "The Velveteen Rabbit" you should. This is just a nib let of the good morsels found in its pages.

I want to expand on the way Jesus makes us Real!

You see, In the beginning of our lives, all of our love and validation comes from others. We form our opinions of ourselves by words spoken over us or to us by others. This makes us "easily breakable, "it makes us "have sharp edges" and to be so fragile that we must "be carefully kept." The truth is "If you live by man's compliments, you will die by their criticism. "

When we learn that God's word matter's more than any compliment, criticism or condemnation. We learn that –

- Our Heavenly Father says Good News about us!
- He says that no matter who our earthly parents are or even if we know them, that our Heavenly Father loves us forever, unconditionally!
- He knows everything about us! Psalm 139:1
- He knew every sin that we would ever make, and He still chose to love us, create us and knit us in our mother's womb! Jeremiah 1:4-5 and Psalm 139:13
- God says we are not a mistake and that all our days are written in His book Psalm 139:15.
- God is not distant and angry, but He is the complete expression of Love! 1 John 4:16
- He wants to give us His Love! 1 John 3:1
- He wants us all to have a Hope and a future! Jeremiah 29:11
- When we are broken hearted, he is close to us! Psalm 34:18

- As a shepherd carries a lamb, He wants to carry us close to His heart Isaiah 40:11

- God loves us so much that He gave Jesus, His son, to die for our sins so that we could be reconciled with God and be part of His Forever Family! 2 Corinthians 5:18-19

- His death on the cross over 2000 years ago was the ONLY SACRIFICE needed to pay for the forgiveness of our sins and for us to be reconciled with God and the resurrected Jesus who sits on the throne of Heaven! 1 John 4:10

- No action is needed other than for us to believe on Him and we will have everlasting life! John 3:16

We who believe on The Son of God – Jesus, have become Real!

"It doesn't happen all at once" "you become. It takes a long time. That's why it" CHANGES PEOPLE "who break easily or have sharp edges or who have to be carefully kept."

We learn that God loves us – REALLY loves us – unconditionally and forever. Because of this we learn to love ourselves, which "Whitney Houston" says is "The greatest Love of all"!

When we learn that we are loveable and forgiven, our hearts soften, and we forgive others. We quit demanding perfection, we quit finding flaws. We learn to delight in the things we have in common and celebrate the differences. We learn coping skills that don't come in a prescription or drug. We learn to breathe in acceptance and not be puppets on a string. We learn to exhale understanding and steadiness with balance. We learn that when we commit our works to the Lord, that He will establish our thoughts. We learn that if we keep His word in our words, thoughts, minds and hearts, that He will establish the works of our hands because we will be pursuing His Will for His Kingdom. We learn that the one true God does not want to replace us but wants to transform us by the renewing of our minds through His word. We learn that we are becoming Real and that we can make a Real difference for Him! We can give back; we can do for others. We can forgive. We can talk to others, not about them. We can learn to work on us! We can learn to live peacefully while at the same time advocating for our own needs appropriately with Love! We can set boundaries; we can remember that God will never ask us to do anything immoral or illegal to please him and that any contract to do anything illegal for that reason is already void.

We have been given a reason to live and serve Jesus! We have life to the fullest! We are no better than anyone else and no one else is any better than us! The ground at the cross is level and in a scale of 1-10 we're all 10's!

Do you want to be Real? Do you believe in Jesus?

Pray

Heavenly Father, thank You for loving me so much that you gave your only son to die in my place so that I could be forgiven, made righteous, and best of all, that I could know you and return your Love! Jesus, if you could love me enough to give your life for me, the least I can do is give my life to you. I believe your blood cleanses me now of all my sin. From now on, I belong to you! Thank you, Holy Spirit, for your presence with me now! Fill me with your Joy and Power so that I can lead others to their Heavenly Father through Jesus Christ. Amen.

I pray for you to be made Real, one day at a time, one moment at a time, one breath at a time and one changed thought at a time drenched in God's sweet words meant for the edification and encouragement of His Body and His Bride!

We who believe in Him are all His Body and His Bride!

Go, love others the way that He loves us!

Always Remember – If God woke you up this morning, say Thanks because He woke you up on Purpose! He has plans for your life!

MY STORY, NO BLAME, NO SHAME!

When I was 16, I had a miscarriage 4-month gestation. I named her Hope. She is in Heaven, and Jesus is the best Daddy anyone can have. When I was 17, I gave birth to a daughter with Down Syndrome. I cherish every moment with her. When I was 19, I gave birth to a son who overcame many obstacles, including ADHD.

Sometime after divorce and life hit, I dabbled in drugs and alcohol. Of course, this was when my kids were teenagers and we lived close to my parents, so they had ample supervision. Since then, I have found many recovery programs, including Celebrate Recovery.

But, at the time, I had given up on life because I could not figure out how to change my life for the better. I surrendered to God. He told me that He is working all the time and He doesn't need us to change the world. BUT that if we are willing, He will equip us and prepare us to change the world in His time, for His story and His Glory!

Today, I work as a Caseworker, managing caseloads. Some of these families have I.E.P.s and I. F. S. P. s, which are Individual Education Plans and Individual Family Service Plans for individuals with special needs. We also serve families who are challenged by Mental Health, addiction, employment issues, and who benefit from our services by learning about jobs, scholarships, getting their records cleared, bonding and opportunities for volunteering or serving on boards.

Last night, I picked up my 9-year chip from Celebrate Recovery. I took a picture of my chip and I shared it on Facebook. A friend of mine that I had previously met at a recovery home congratulated me on it. She told me that it gives Hope to others and You never know who may be watching, and the inspiration is touching lives.

God spoke to me right then, He told me that He would show me how He uses EVERY pain and trial as the very thing that equips us and prepares us to change the world for the better for His Story and His Glory!

Then, she said, you are a Hope Dealer!

My friend, every time I share my story, I bring Hope to life and give meaning to every second of my family's life with redemption, No Blame, No Shame for the Glory of God!

God is no respecter of person's what He does for one, He will do for all who are willing.

BROKEN

I am a broken vessel. A cracked pot. A sinner with tattoos, but all this can be used as my testimony.

Now when I meet someone who has brokenness in their life caused by pain from something I have gone through – be it my mother when she passed away from breast cancer, the loss of Hope in more ways than 1, drugs, nightmares, living hell on earth. I can say hallelujah! I know just who to call or just what scriptures to stand on praise the lord we can walk through this together. I tell them I took that class, and I chose to major in Praise and worship to the 1 true God. It is the only foundation that can weather life's storms.

When I separated from my husband, I had to begin a new relationship with Jesus Christ. I don't know where he found you, but he pulled me straight from the pit of hell on earth! Not worshipping the 1 true God had opened so many doors that the demons that tormented me somehow gained the power to hurt me physically. My Health Care Provider didn't know what to think!

I finally became broken and called out to God for him to show himself. He then sent people in my path that showed his love, not criticism and condemnation. I want to thank my friends and counselors for their guidance and help to break the soul ties to my past. I also want to thank my churches for their prayer covering. And I want to thank Celebrate Recovery for helping me find friends that I can identify with.

During the time of my separation, I called out to Jesus to be my Husband and my provider. I had had a stroke and could not work. My blood pressure was 196/96. I claimed His provision and stood on His promises. God allowed me to get disability. Praise the Lord. I now had time to work on mine and Jesus' relationship and my life! I quit smoking and had the gastric bypass surgery to lose weight. Since then, I have lost 80 lbs and my blood pressure is 110/70. I do not have to take insulin, high blood pressure or high cholesterol medicine anymore. My mental health is stable!

I know that Jesus is my provider, and he is with me wherever I go. If the devil or his demons try to harass me on the job, I send Jesus to the door. This is not my fight but His. Jesus is alive and well and he is performing miracles every day in my life, and he can do the same for you.

I want you to know that it hasn't been easy – in the beginning I came to Jesus and started going to church dirty! I was still getting high and living in sin! I said God, I can't do this on my own, you are going to have to clean me by your might because my will is not strong enough. I can't stay clean, I can't stay pure, I can't show the love of Jesus. God's word says – Ezekiel 36:27 I will put my spirit within you, I will enable you to live by my laws, and you will obey my rules. Hebrews 8:10 -12 This is the covenant I will make with the house of Israel after that time, declares the Lord, I will put my laws in their minds and write them in their hearts for I will forgive their wickedness and will remember their sins no more.

Every day is my 2 day. A day that I get to try to do better than I did the day before, and on the 3rd day, the same spirit that rose Jesus from the dead will rise up in me and overcome any struggle that I am going through.

Satan cannot overcome us, but he tries to discourage us through his lies – I choose from now on not to agree with him. I am a child of God saved by grace, through faith an heir of eternal life, Forgiven and led by the spirit of God, a new creature redeemed from the curse of the law, kept in safety wherever I go, strong in the Lord and his mighty power, Living by faith and not by sight, rescued from the dominion of darkness, justified blest with every spiritual blessing, an overcomer by the blood of the Lamb and the word of my testimony, the light of the world, healed by his wounds, being transformed by the renewing of my mind, and heir to the blessings of Abraham, doing all things thru Christ who gives me strength, I am more than a conqueror thru Jesus Christ, ALL praise, honor and glory belongs to him! Poem by Clyde Weigel.

Helpful prayer – strengthen me 2 stand up knowing you are always with me, Fall fresh on me today so I can find my joy and peace again. Restore the broken places in my life. I want to have the resources and love required to provide for me and my family. I desire the energy and motivation to perform my job and daily task at home. Give me a fresh breeze of release to lighten my load. Teach me your way and your will. Speak to me Lord in a way that I would understand and obey. Send the right people in my life to be a source of love, guidance, and new opportunities. Thank you, Jesus, for your Mercy and Grace. Thank you for Favor in this season. I am ready for serenity and solutions to adapt to the changes in my life. I thank you now in advance because I believe you are an awesome God instead of wishing, whining, weeping, feeling weak, weary, and worried – I will worship my way back to wholeness. Instead of a breakdown I am ready for my breakthrough. Thank you, Lord, for leading me to this prayer that speaks to my heart and strengthens my faith in you. I am ready for my healing and deliverance. Thank you, Lord, for working it out. It is so. It is done. It is well with my soul. I exhale now trusting you Lord as I walk away from temptation, depression, and all the strongholds of the enemy. Your divine Law operates within me with your protection and your provision. My trust in you Lord allows me to exhale the stress, worry and shame. Divine Spirit, I am encouraged now and will press on in the name of Jesus, Amen.

THE CRISIS PREGNANCY CENTER

I hope that when you read this you see Jesus and his love for us all.

When I was 16, I had a spontaneous miscarriage at 4 months Gestation. I named it Hope.

When I was 17, I got pregnant again. My Mom told me that her insurance would pay for an abortion.

I called the abortion clinic and made an appointment. I broke down and cried, I could not go through with it.

When I was 17, I graduated High School, got married, bought a house, and had a baby. Not in that order!

I had a little girl and I love her dearly.

When I was 19, I got pregnant again. My marriage was going through a trial. I made another abortion appointment.

I went to the Crisis Pregnancy Center. They did a pregnancy test and gave me a life size plastic baby the size of a baby 4-month gestation. Right then and there I said that there is no way that I'm having the abortion ever!

I had my little boy that year.

God honored my decision to keep my kids regardless of if I had a steady job at the time or any full proof plans and He provided for me and mine.

I now have grandkids that I get to share my life with and make memories that would have never been possible if I had had either abortion.

We survived! God created each of us to be survivors and warriors!

On Facebook every year, on October 15th, Facebook promotes a worldwide day to celebrate the lives of all babies and kids who have gone on to be with the Lord (my terminology).

Guess What? My first grandson's birthday is October 15th!

My hope is in Jesus, Jesus lives in me! My Hope is never lost! I am never forsaken!

Heavenly Father: You hold all things. You hold our past, present, and future. When I face a bleak outlook, a difficult wait, or an intimidating foe, please remind me that you are in charge. You can turn the tables. You can bring about the unexpected. You can make the impossible possible. And God, with you, there is always Hope! Thank you, Lord Jesus Christ! In Jesus name, I pray, Amen!

Discernment

I was told if you are good, you will only hear God's voice... that is not true. Eve heard the devil's voice, and she was in the most protected place on earth - The Garden of Eden.

Jesus heard the voice of Satan in the wilderness. Satan even used scripture. Jesus combatted it with the truth of the scripture.

There will be voices ... audible voices... from other people, or voices in your head ... from thoughts ... etc.

These are voices that you have to choose how to react to.

When you hear a voice ... or a thought, don't automatically react to it ... Take a minute to process it ... compare it to the truths in God's word.

If you accept a belief – you reap a thought; If you sow a thought – you reap an attitude, if you sow an attitude - you reap an action. If you sow an action – you reap a habit, if you sow a habit, you reap a character, if you sow a character – you reap a destiny. Take care because your beliefs grow into your destiny! (COPIED OFF OF FACEBOOK)

If Satan can get you to believe his lie on any 1 of these steps, he can make you feel like a loser who has no hope and whose god is small. You are a blood bought child of the king of kings and you can choose today to not be intimidated by this tactic of the devil.

Satan might have told you things like "you're not like everyone else," or "you're crazy," or things that make you believe that the voice that is telling you to do illegal or immoral things that you are hearing really is a god. It might be a god, but if it is not God. Everybody always says to discern. But no-one taught me how!

The devil is a fallen angel who is very deceiving and who already tricked one third of all the angels. If he is after you – be sure that you have a God given call on your life that he wants to deceive you into believing that you are not equipped or qualified for. The enemy wouldn't be attacking you if something very valuable wasn't inside of You. Thieves don't break into empty houses. You've got a purpose! You are no match for the enemy, but Jesus has already defeated him, and if you are born again, he lives in you. Therefore, the victory has already been won! The next time you hear a voice listen to what its message is and use this chart to determine from whence it came.

God	**Satan**
Stills you	Rushes you
Reassures you	Frightens you
Leads you	Pushes you
Enlightens you	Confuses you
Forgives you	Condemns you
Calms you	Stresses you
Encourages you	Discourages you
Comforts you	Worries you

YOU CAN CHOOSE WHICH VOICE TO LISTEN TO TODAY!

Not only does this tell you who to believe, but it tells you so much about the type of love God really has for you! He wants the best for you at all times – even while you are sinning! Favor comes before the obedience!

My God is a loving and forgiving God who loves us and only wants to give us a hope and a future! He will establish us! 2 Thessalonians 3:3 But the Lord is faithful, who shall establish you, and guard you from the evil one.

OTHER VOICES

You will also have to determine whose advice to take and whose voice to listen to – just remember God never commanded you to trust people. God commanded you to love people and TRUST HIM! Know the difference. Your Joy & Victory depend on it!

I have been through Hell on earth, I have been raped, abused, neglected and abandoned. But God! I have been through the hurt of divorce and separation. BUT GOD!

At one time, I had a lot of un-forgiveness in my heart. This fact disabled me and kept me bound inside my house and inside my head. Isolation is 1 of the devils' main tactics. If he can get you all alone with only his voices to listen to or the thoughts he puts in your head, then he has you all to himself to torture and torment as much as he sees fit.

There In my pain – I called out to God - I said show yourself to me– I then chased whoever showed me the most power. I thought they were God! Then in my shock and disbelief – the most powerful people fell and showed their humanness, and I was led back to the name above all names Jesus Christ!

Finally, Jesus led me to people who didn't use my label to view me through – but told me that there was an answer!

I got in the word of God – Psalms 90:17 And let the favor of the Lord our God be upon us; And establish thou the work of our hands; yea, the work of our hands establish thou it.

. . .

I have a Bachelor's Degree in Psychology. All my life I had been searching for an answer. But when I got to the end of my learning as a psychology student – I was still faced with the same questions.

-What is the difference in someone who believes in God and hears his voice, versus someone who hears voices who is a schizophrenic?

-Is there help for someone who grew up in a dysfunctional family?

Psychology teaches us that in a dysfunctional family there is a rescuer, a scapegoat, a lost child, a mascot, and various members of the family share the role of enabler.

In a dysfunctional family there are 5 rolls:

The Hero or rescuer – usually an older child who assumes the role of the responsible 1.

The Scapegoat – the child who gets blamed for the family's problems. Finding the hero roll already taken – this child sees acting out as the only way of getting attention.

The lost child - never make waves – ignores the family's problem – the chameleon – blends into surroundings

The mascot – makes a joke out of everything – majors in fixing people's feelings.

The enabler – "the wife of a drug addict that keeps the family secret."

I learned all about these rolls and how they function in a dysfunctional family, only to find out that - That was the end of Psychology. That's as far as it took me. I felt like there was no answer except to find your roll and play it as well as you could so that everyone in your family could feel needed in their roll.

I was so disappointed – I wanted to provide my children with more than that. I knew the statistic's – most people who grew up in a so-called dysfunctional family pass those behaviors on to their children.

I learned coping mechanisms through self-help books and church. After the voices and thoughts had quieted down and I could actually think, God showed me that there indeed was an answer.

I learned that I could make a change that would be a permanent one that would impact my family and how we relate to each other forever. I learned that I could unlearn dysfunctional behavior and learn functional behavior. God says that by me learning and showing new, more appropriate behaviors and practicing them, would teach my family that it is possible and therefore change their beliefs and behaviors.

For the 1st time in years I had found a glimmer of Hope!

I am not perfect. I am a sinner. I have a past. Sometimes I feel like I'm the messiest person in the room. But, regardless of all of this, God has never stopped loving me and He never will!

I found out that I had to get to the end of my understanding to get to the beginning of God's. Only God can provide lasting change. Only through the love and forgiveness of His Son Jesus Christ can true relationships begin. I began my relationship with Jesus, and He taught me how to begin a real relationship with my children and my family. A relationship that teaches everyone involved how to feel, trust, and to talk to each other. I had to learn that I am loved even when I mess up or make a mistake. I had to learn that in order to show that to my family.

2 Corinthians 1:3-4 Blessed be the God and Father of our Lord Jesus Christ, the father of all mercies, & God of all comfort, who comforts us in all our affliction so that we may be able to comfort those who are in any affliction <u>with the comfort with which we ourselves are comforted by God.</u>

I now can have open, honest, and loving relationships. I learned how to give and receive constructive criticism with an open mind, without giving or taking offense. I have developed relationships that are more authentic. Pat Springle says "authentic relationships are based on honest communication, respect for one another's separateness, and genuine love." He says "the growth that accompanies recovery frees us from being imprisoned by hurt, bitterness, shame, and manipulation." Hallelujah!

Because of God's propitiation, I felt forgiven **and that changed** how I could relate to others. I immediately forgave them and quit demanding perfection for my love. I quit expecting my payback for my good deeds to come from who I gave it to. I do everything for God and expect my payback or blessings to come from Him! This led to less resentment in my life.

Resentment can equal un-forgiveness, and un-forgiveness is an open doorway for Satan to have access into your life to torment you.

I quit speaking negative things over my family out loud –to anyone. I pray to God about the person. He already knows the situation. But I didn't give another person or the devil any ammunition to use against me or my family.

– just remember God never commanded you to trust people. God commanded you to love people and TRUST HIM! Know the difference. Your Joy & Victory depend on it!

I found the friend that I always wanted to walk hand in hand with me through all of life's struggles – because the struggle is real –and you can't do life alone!

I found out that God was there with me even when I tried to run to the world for answers. I found out that **He is the Answer**.

I am loved even when I mess up or make a mistake. He will rescue me from the dominion of darkness. He will redeem me from the curse of the Law. He will establish me, and He will give me a Hope and a Future. He will do the same for you. There is Hope! There is an answer – His name is Jesus Christ, and He is the name above all names! He is alive and active in my life, and He can be in yours!

God	**Satan**
Stills you	Rushes you
Reassures you	Frightens you
Leads you	Pushes you
Enlightens you	Confuses you
Forgives you	Condemns you
Calms you	Stresses you
Encourages you	Discourages you
Comforts you	Worries you

I believe in God the Father, God the son, and God the Holy Spirit. I believe that no mortal can take their place. They are spiritual beings, and they live in us, the ones who have asked them into our hearts. I rely on the Father, the Son, and the Holy Spirit to guide my thoughts and actions. There is nothing immoral or illegal about the Holy Trinity. The Holy Trinity will never guide you to do anything immoral or illegal. Jesus is the son of the Living God, but He is a Heavenly creature not a mortal being.

The same spirit that raised Jesus from the dead lives in us. I believe that God can resurrect anyone He wants to at any time.

We live, move and in Him we have our being. We are forgiven, loved, chosen, and cherished by the most - high God!

Real true God kind of love is unconditional, it is not

competitive, it is not critical. It is not judgmental. It is not greedy.

Love one another and Love God as He has loved you!

The one true God loves us all unconditionally, He does not want to replace us, but He wants to transform us by the renewing of our minds through scripture and true unconditional love.

One day at a time, be happy in the now, celebrate you!

Isolation –
1 of Satan's deadliest strongholds

Even in the Garden of Eden – God's most protected place on earth – God chose to allow Adam & Eve to have free will. This included chances to sin willfully. Satan waited until Eve was alone and isolated to tempt her. He came to her in the form of a serpent, 1 of God's created animals!

She heard his voice - she had a conversation with him. Belonging to God does not mean that you won't hear the devil's voice or that you will never be tempted. Even Jesus was visited by the father of lies and tempted. We must learn to respond to that voice by discernment and the Word of God.

Even Lions, when they hunt their prey, they wait until they can separate one from the pack. Then they pounce. This is how they can take down huge elephants or giraffes bigger than them. Isolation is a tactic of Satan. If he can isolate you and get you away from your friends who believe in Jesus. If he can get you alone and lonely, then it is easier for you to fall into a sin that disguises itself as a good time. After you sin, he can keep you isolated by condemning you and causing guilt and shame. This keeps you hiding and isolating. Now he is the only voice you hear and he has you where he wants you.

The only answer is to get in The Word of God and combat his lies with it. We live not by bread alone but by every word that comes out of the mouth of God. We must keep godly people around us and make more time for them. Ask a few people to be your prayer partners. Write down your prayers and find scriptures to go with them so that you will be praying according to God's will. Write down your miracles as they come as answers to your prayers.

Satan will try to get you offended just to isolate you again. Be wise to his tactics and don't let him win. Pray that you can live and work without giving or taking offense. Forgive and keep open lines of communication. Talk about things. Build relationships. Have bonding moments. Build a foundation that can weather the storms. Jesus is the answer.

Satan has tactics but God has the power. We have to choose to be grateful. "Liberty lies in the hearts of men and women; when it dies there, no constitution, no law, no court can save it. Proverbs 15:15 All the days of the oppressed are wretched, BUT the cheerful heart has a continual feast.

God's power is not intimidated by your circumstances. You are empowered by God to reach & accomplish goals that transcend human limitations!

Psalms 90:17 & let the favor of the Lord our God be upon us; & establish thou the work of our hands; yea, the work of our hands establish thou it!

. . .

(copied from Facebook)

Jesus will go before you and He will send His angels and His spirit and His people before you - He will change the world to equip you in your time.

"God does not give us overcoming life: he gives us life as we overcome."

"Pray that God will rain down His restoration to smooth over the dirt road and make new trails of freedom in Christ for you."

FAITH

I have finally found the SUBSTANCE that I was born to be addicted to ... My bible says that "Faith is the substance of things hoped for and the evidence of things unseen." FAITH is the belief that God will change your life, the definition of Faith is - the complete trust or confidence in someone or something (God).

...... One day, I woke up terrified, anxious, depressed, weary and thought the end was near. Another nightmare sent from the devil to attempt to keep me from God's divine guidance. I had heard what others said about it...I decided to see what God said about it.

HE said "FEAR NOT, neither be thou dismayed, for it is I the Lord your God who holds your right hand, it is I who say to you, FEAR NOT, it is I who help you, I go before you to prepare a place for you, I will make the crooked places straight and I will put a song in your heart. I will never leave you nor forsake you, put your Faith in the Power of God, <u>not the wisdom of man</u>, for I am with you always, forgive, love, and encourage, encourage, encourage even more as we see the day approaching, for in Christ, old things are passed away and behold all things become new, and if any man be in Christ, he is a new creature and there is now no condemnation in Christ."

"<u>Now turn again and help your brother, but be careful lest ye should fall</u>, put away the pointing of the finger and the tongue, for all have sinned and come short of the Glory of God, let the words of my mouth and the meditation of our hearts be acceptable in your sight Oh Lord."

God inhabits the Praises of His people; the new heaven and new earth will be filled only with Praises. Praises of God and Praises of His people.

When you truly love someone, like Jesus loved you, you can praise them

-call out the positives and pray that God handles the rest. That's what prayer is for.

IF SOMEONE TELLS YOU THEY HAVE A PAST, KNOW THAT GOD IS A FORGIVING AND A LOVING GOD. WE ALL HAVE A PAST AND WE ALL HAVE VOICES THAT MOLD OUR LIVES, ALL THAT MATTERS IS WHICH ONE WE ARE GOING TO LISTEN TO TODAY!

There is a season for everyone and everything. We are not God, so we have no idea what that person was put on this earth to help someone through, and we don't have any idea what they are supposed to go through before God is ready for them. Sometimes, when we play God and judge them when they are going through their trials, we are failing to realize that WE are the very thing that God put in their path to bring them to Him. AND WE HAVE TO GET OVER OUR JUDGEMENTS OF THEM IN ORDER TO LOVE THEM.

There is a book called "My Father Is A Woman and My Mother Is Black" True story. The author of the story was in special education all her life, and only her special education teacher could read her writing but helped her to publish that book. PROVING THAT AGAIN... THERE ARE POSSIBIL-ITIES IN EVERYONE!

I know multiple people who are living testimonies of how God redeemed them from a bad childhood, including molesta-tion, abuse, neglect, divorce, drugs, alcohol, etc.

Be the miracle... Bad things happen, even to good people... Only when we incorporate our experiences and struggles into our testimony with redemption can GOD use us and anoint us to serve others not by knowing how to solve their problems or that they have some...but by taking their hand and walking through it with them.

The anointing is for service. If we want the anointing, then we must get over the fact that we have a GIFT and start being the GIFT. IT'S NOT ABOUT THE GIFT YOU HAVE, IT'S ABOUT THE GIFT YOU ARE.

If someone comes to you for help - they don't need condemnation. They already know they have a problem they are alone and feeling under the circumstances...They need to be led to God's Love, Mercy and Grace. Help them to help them-selves. Encourage them enough so that they believe in them-selves enough to handle today's stress and they might handle tomorrows! Don't talk about them, don't talk around them like they can't hear you. LISTEN, PRAY, PUT AWAY THE POINTING OF THE FINGER AND THE TONGUE! Treat them like they were Jesus in disguise and pray that God handles their issues. Then we can plant our seeds and expect a harvest.

Identify - Jesus came to identify with all of us -in that he died on the cross - each of us have a cross to bear - he can identify - he has been there -and he still loves us JUST AS WE ARE.

IT TOOK PEOPLE WHO WERE WILLING TO STEP OUT IN FAITH TO LOVE ME JUST LIKE I WAS, IN THE CIRCUMSTANCE I WAS IN, NO MATTER WHAT, AND THEN AND ONLY THEN DID I LEARN THAT GOD REALLY DID EXIST BECAUSE LOVE EXIST...AND GOD IS LOVE. I DON'T CARE WHAT THE ISSUE IS... PLANT YOUR SEED AND PRAY THAT GOD HANDLES THE REST.

Religion, legalist condemnation would tell you that you have a right to be GOD and judge or decipher right and wrongs. Beware, religious people are who killed Jesus. Don't fall prey to this. Leave it in God's hands. Forgive, do your part.

SOMETIMES JUST ONE STORY OF HOPE CAN ELIMINATE THE CYCLE OF HATE IN AN ENTIRE FAMILY GENERATION. LET'S KEEP HOPE ALIVE FOR THIS GENERATION AND THE NEXT. I HAVE FAITH IN YOU, AND I BELIEVE IN YOU.

I am committed to Jesus, because He has established me and has given me and my family new purpose and hope for the future, while helping me gain stability in my life.

We can never give up on helping family members and

friends reclaim their lives _ WE HAVE NO IDEA HOW MANY LIVES ARE COUNTING ON THEM.

When you help others, God fights your battles. His word says that "For whosoever shall give you a cup of water to drink in my name, because he/they belong to Christ, verily I say unto you, he/they shall not lose his/their reward.

I WILL SEND THEE

In 1995, I went to Japan with Fuji Photo Film to start up a new plant. We went for training since the only plants they had running were there. We were there a little over 2 months. Right before I went, there was an earthquake in a little place called Kobe, Japan. The name Kobe means God's Doorway. Automatically, I knew this was God's way of letting me know that he would be going with me. His word says "I will be with thee where ever thou go."

On March 20th, 1995, my daughter's 5th birthday, we were in Tokyo, we were about to take the subway when someone had the idea to return to Kita kami on the romance car. The romance car is a train where you can sit in the very front and see everything. The entire front of the train is glass. We all decided to go on the romance car. It was later that evening when we found out that there had been a bombing in Tokyo on the subway! The phone lines for all of Japan were shut down for three days. I couldn't receive or make calls. My family didn't even know if I was alive for three days. But thanks to God, I was able to make a late Happy Birthday call! I had been inches away from death without even knowing it, someone must've been praying!

I know that my life was saved for a purpose and that God has a plan for me.

I really loved Japan, it was breathtakingly beautiful, everywhere you looked you could see mountains covered with snow. They had carp fish that looked like huge goldfish swimming in the river along the walkways. They had temples, shrines and castles everywhere.

I did find God there, but I kept him to myself. I did not follow his word and share the good news.

Upon return to America, my Mother taught English as a second language to the Japanese and we learned how to cook many Japanese dishes. I have been asked to come back to Japan to visit the families we shared memories with. I believe that God will open up doors again.

Valerie, a friend of mine, recently went to China on a teaching assignment. She shared the good news and created a bible study for other teachers there - they asked her to come back, she will be able to continue to let her light shine. What a testimony!

Valerie taught me something about God and God taught me something about himself. He can be where you are, but if you do not follow his commandments, speak forth His word and pray and teach and share the good news, then you are wasting your time and opening up yourself and your life up to the destruction done by people who do not serve Him. No matter where you are!

He opens doors for us to share His love and our testimonies every day, it's up to us to get out of our comfort zones and choose not to settle for anything less than His pure love, forgiveness, grace and mercy to get us through. He wants this love to show through us wherever we are. We don't just go to church - we are the church; Jesus is living on the inside of us and can manifest his healing powers in all aspects of our lives if we let him and invite him in! When you are in His will, windows of opportunity arise out of His divine appointment with His protection and His provision.

OPPORTUNITYISNOWHERE! What do you see? Now Here or Nowhere?

I now have a new purpose, In the future, I plan on using further chances to travel to further the Kingdom of Heaven. I now spend time in His word so that it is a lamp unto my feet and a light unto my heart.

Karen Wheaton says that "When you do sow into this generation, you will reap in the blessings for your own family." When you do for others, God does for you and yours!

Showing my Faith does not mean I am weak or gullible! It means I have divine protection and provision in my life and it also means that I don't open doors for people not in his will to bring destruction into my life that would cause harm.

If need be, I am not afraid to call his appointed protectors here on earth into my life to make sure my family is always in a place of protection. I am a blood bought child of the King of Kings. I have nothing getting in the way of me calling for protection on earth or in Heaven. That leaves no room for the enemy to attempt to control me anymore. I make it a point not to allow someone to put me in harm's way by their presence in my life.

The love of Jesus has taught me that I am loved and treasured and important to Him. If I am important to Him, then I have a right to stand up for myself. It matters to Him and therefore it matters to me. That's true for you too! You are important to Him. You matter to Him. WE HAVE A RIGHT TO STAND UP FOR OURSELVES. Don't allow hurtful people in your environment. If they have to be there, then maybe God has put you in that position to teach them better ways.

Learn how to give and receive constructive criticism without giving or taking offense. Learn how to have the tough conversations! You will grow from it!

But... in the end we don't have to have man's acceptance - If you live by man's compliments you will die by their criticisms.

I live by God's words.

Fear evaporates & hope springs up as we encounter The risen Lord!

We can call on Him to defend us. 1 Samuel 24:12 Jehovah judge between me and thee; but my hand shall not be upon thee.

Psalm 46:10 says "Be still & know that I am God."

Trust that He will handle all of your issues and outcomes.

My favorite 1

Isaiah 49:25 & 26 But this saith the Lord, even the captives of the mighty shall be taken away, & the prey of the terrible shall be delivered: for I will contend with him that contendeth with thee, and I will save thy children & I will feed them that oppress thee with their own flesh; and they shall be drunken with their own blood as with sweet wine and all flesh shall know that I the Lord am thy savior.

"May 19th,2014 Today God's message for you is to know that you are not a human being seeking spirituality, but a spiritual being seeking humanness. As that one spirit, you alone can invoke changes to the human race. As that human spirit, you can help build bridges and move mountains for the betterment of humankind."

"June 12th, 2014 Today God's message for you Is to make the most of your time on earth. Be able to look back on your day with satisfaction as you lay your head down to sleep. Think of the relationships you honed, the conversations you had, the lives you may have changed and the way it all may have changed you. It was time well spent."

"July 15th,2014 God's Daily Message Today God's message for you is to release fear. Though life provides difficulties to strengthen your spirits, you do not face them alone. God is with you, beside you and surrounding you. He will provide all the help you need, He will hold you up! His source of comfort, security & infinite love knows no end!"

Isaiah 60:14-22 Violence shall no more be heard in thy land, wasting nor destruction with-in the borders; but thou shalt call thy walls salvation, and thy gates praise. The sun shall be no more thy light by day; neither for brightness shall the moon give light to thee but the Lord shall be unto thee an everlasting light, & thy God the glory. Thy sun shall no more go down, neither shall thy moon withdraw itself: for the Lord shall be thine everlasting light & the days of thy mourning shall be ended. Thy people also shall be all righteous: they shall inherit the land forever, the branch of my planting, the work of my hands, that I may be glorified. A little one shall become a thousand, and a small one a strong nation: I the Lord will hasten it in His time.

Colossians 1:17 He is before all things and in Him all things hold together.

Deuteronomy 30:19 & 20 I call heaven & earth to record this day against you, that I have set before you life and death, blessing and cursing, therefore choose life, that both thou and thy seed may live.

1 Peter 5:10 And the God of all grace, who called you to his eternal glory in Christ, after you have suffered a little while, will himself restore you and make you strong, firm and steadfast.

I AM NOT AN ORPHAN

My Dad is in Heaven now with my Mom and my baby Hope. I know that they now have their healthy, heavenly body. I gained Angels. I am a child of God and I have been adopted into his heavenly family. Even better, so has my family.

Now I know that I can and will rely on my Heavenly Father to never leave me or forsake me as it says in His Word. Jesus is my husband and my provider. I am loved. I am adopted. I am chosen. I am adored. I have a life worth living. I sometimes make mistakes, but God turns them into His messages.

I am a supporter of the semicolon project. A semicolon is put into a sentence when the author has decided instead of putting a period and ending the sentence; they choose to continue the story. The author is Jesus.

And, because of His love, I choose to continue my story! I have a Hope and a future!

I love my family, I can't make us perfect, but I can try to keep us stable and structured and clean and fed.

I can try to have caring friends who want the best for me and my family.

I can try to make the best relationships out of the ones we have.

I can try to keep my family together as one team. While also becoming part of our community in a healthy way.

I have a past, but I'm saved. I am the righteousness of Christ and it is not I that lives but Christ who lives in me. Jesus can make our mistakes into a message that gives us purpose. When it is our purpose to give Him Glory, He will defend and protect us. We are made in Christ image, because of this we were born with everything already inside of us that we will ever need.

I break the chains of generational curses on our families. I ask forgiveness for our past. I ask for unity and love and proper boundaries and behavior that shows the fruits of the spirit. Stability in foundations, deep roots, support systems and fellowship. We are blessed and have resurrection power restoring our relationships. We have been made whole by the unconditional love and forgiveness of the name above all names Jesus Christ. May our worship be constant, and our praise be inhabited by your presence always. May all our families be a house of prayer.

You are free so be quick to forgive.

Forgiveness is a choice and decision of your will so choose to forgive.

We are purified and washed as we forgive our offenders;

therefore, determine to live every day with a forgiving spirit as the offenses come.

Capture those thoughts and replace them with good thoughts

Nothing can separate us from His great love.

I used to believe the devil's lies. I thought that you had to become someone who you are not for you to be new. I don't have to replace someone else! You cannot replace me! The minute you believe the lie that you are someone else, you lose your own identity! That is a trick of the enemy to steal, kill and destroy. That is a trick of others to steal your identity and make you feel lost. Fight for your identity. Fight for your life. You are loved, your identity is that you are a child of God. No one can take that away from you because Jesus will never leave you or forsake you. Be the best YOU that you can be.

If you want to go somewhere fast, go alone! If you want to go far, go together!

I got a personal word in 2004, many people have received words that we are being trained to pray, build, grow, and go far, Together!

To be successful, let's not let the Devil divide, conquer and stop God's agenda and call anymore. We are here to lead others to Jesus Christ. We catch them, He cleans them! That's what He does!

Unity is the only Church and the only way we can ever build and be part of the Church that the gates of Hell will not prevail against!

If you look for faults, you will find them!

Cast your cares on Jesus, because He cares for us!

Religion is about exclusivity. Playing God! Jesus Christ tells us to love as He loves! He loves all unconditionally and forever! Being servants of the one true God.

The one true God does not want to replace anyone, like the world tries to do, but He wants to transform us by the renewing of our minds through the Word of God that will stand forever.

My bible says that we are all loved, chosen, brand new, forgiven, and cherished.

I have a call on my life and I believe you do too! The gifts and callings of God are irrevocable.

I want to be part of what God is doing. I will. Will you?

No matter where you come from, He can heal you. He can make you whole and strong. In my past, not recent past, but my past, I have been bullied, beaten, raped, neglected, and abandoned.

But I was never alone in my journey. God never left my side, He never quit loving me. I have never broken a bone in my body. He

Has held me. Jesus is my husband and my provider, my healer, and my restorer. He is my everything. Everyone else is a lesson or a blessing. God is resurrecting Hope in many ways in my life. He lives in me, and He lives in you. I am amazed at all He does. There is no name above Jesus. Lives matter to Him. Thanks for giving me a chance to praise Him. I love my church family; God bless us everyone.

GALATIANS 35:35 HE HAS FILLED EACH OF US WITH SKILLS

I n Jesus, all things hold together!

We are all valuable human beings that deserve to be respected and loved.

I am the first to admit that I am not perfect, and I have a past. But I am forgiven because Jesus died on the cross for ALL of us 2000 years ago and no further sacrifice is needed for any of us to be forgiven.

I am a Mom. I am a Nanna, I am a sister, I am a daughter, I am an aunt, I am an employee, I am a friend, I am part of the body of Christ, and I am a daughter of the Most-High!

Each child of God is valuable to God! We are not paychecks, we are not slaves, we are not property, we cannot be sold, traded, or bartered!

Our identity is our own!

Our identity is found in the love that God has for us. He alone is our rock. No other substance can have power over us or our thoughts. His word teaches us to overcome respectfully.

Showing the love of Jesus. Knowing that regardless of our happenings, we can be happy. Knowing without a doubt, that He will never leave us or forsake us and that He wants the best for us always.

No weapon formed against us will prosper and everything that the devil tries to harm us with, God will turn around for His glory and our story and testimony of His strength and protection.

Our joy and happiness require that we have this intimate, no cost relationship with our heavenly father, Abba. Because of that, He will hold all things pertaining to our lives in His divine order.

He is before all things, He is in all things, and because of Him all things exist. In Him all things hold together.

WE ARE THE BRIDE OF CHRIST

T his means that He remains forever true and faithful and will supply all our needs according to His riches in glory. He will never leave us or forsake us, and we are never alone. We are His beloved and He will protect us and keep us in His will. The scripture says that if we keep His words in our hearts, He will give us the desires of our hearts and that we can ask, and it shall be given to us. He will sustain us and cause us to live in peaceful habitation.

Our callings and God given purpose are irrevocable. If God calls us to it, He will provide and He will guide. It is for a purpose. Everything we do leaves an impact on the future. Make it good.

I ask for God to open the doors that He wants open and to close the doors that He wants to shut. When He opens a door, no man can shut it.

He guides us, He sustains us, He rescues us, He provides a

way of escape, He gives us courage and strength, motivation, and discernment when we ask for it.

Our value is not defined by whether we are married or single. Our value is based on to whom we belong. We belong to God.

God is a heavenly being. A Holy Spirit. An immortal authority that cannot be defined by mortal standards. God cannot be manufactured or contained. God does not change. GOD IS.

It is not up to any man or woman to keep hold of our lives or our kid's lives. We cannot lose anything that is in God's hands. God loves us all the same. There is nothing we can do to become loved in His eyes. We are chosen by God. We are loved. We are valued. We are the Bride of Christ; we are His beloved. We are deeply cherished by the creator of the universe.

Contentment is Gain

I have a daughter who was born with Down Syndrome, and I believe that she is perfectly like the Lord Jesus Christ wants her to be at this time. I believe that she is healed by the stripes of Jesus, and I believe that my faith is established. The fact that she has Down Syndrome does not mean that my faith is lacking.

I take medicine. I feel like God is in charge and He provides all the care that is available to us and the fact that we are always available to him as messengers of his love in all situations means: that he needed someone in our position at this time. Therefore, he has sent us.

This is what I believe, faith is acting on what you believe. You must act on what you believe to get results. Price says that you need to be very careful about what you believe, because what you believe is what you are going to act upon. And what you act upon is what you are going to get. I could believe that God healed my daughter and invited a "perfect stranger" in as my daughter if I wanted to show worldly perfection. Worldly perfection is not always gain nor is it always in my best interest. The only truly perfect person is Jesus Christ. I was not created to show perfection. I was created to show God's amazing strength through my weaknesses. That is where his divine power shows through. I don't want to lead people to my perfection but to His.

"My goal is to live by the Spirit of God." "Be wise as serpents and harmless as doves." "God is going to confirm his word with signs and following. The power of God will come into play and move things out of the way."

I have been healed of lung cancer. The power of God literally healed my body of it. The dr. said I had a mass show up on x-ray. I prayed and plead the blood of Jesus over it. 6 months later I had a tube stuck down my throat in surgery that showed no mass. Praise the Lord.

I still take medications for various things – there is no lack of faith – there is no contradiction. I believe that my God will provide all my needs according to his riches in Glory. Right now, God has a purpose for my life, and he has positioned me to be right where I am to show his glory and his power. I am where I am because he is who is he is. I have spoken to objects of debt-I have had student loans, etc. to be totally paid off in Jesus' name and further education provided by God almighty.

I know that God has not given me a spirit of fear but of power, love, and a sound mind. I step out in Faith every day for God to provide for me. He has provided this job. He will provide. He is the God of all weeks.

Don't lose hope! No losses!

When you listen to the lies of the devil, it is easy to lose Hope!

When people are in constant competition for their healing, it causes extreme and intense competition for life. God is a big God and he is no respecter of persons. What He does for one person, he can do for all! He does not play favorites.

Sometimes people seem to point fingers at others for sinning differently than them. The truth is that when we find fault, it is impossible to find something that God does not already know about or that would make God not love anyone or turn His back on them. Usually, fault finding is jealousy in action to try to manipulate favoritism.

People have their opinions and favorites, but every day, God loves each of us into unique wholeness when we rely on Him.

He is the author and creator of life.

God loves us just like we are, in our sin and mess! God wants us, He will clean us and restore us to sanity. We belong to Him. He is God and He has all authority, He can resurrect anyone he chooses at any time and in any way He sees fit. He corrects us, He cleans us, and He saves us. He redeems us, He heals us, He sanctifies us, He purifies us. He sent his son to die for us and no further sacrifice is needed for us to be forgiven and free! We can make a conscious decision to do the right thing, even if we have made mistakes in the past. Today, we can live a new life.

We do have a Hope and a future, We are chosen. We should pray every-day to be delivered from the snare of the fowler. We must have discernment and not fall prey to those who set traps for others to fall into because of their own hurt and pain. We must be wise as serpents and harmless as doves. God will always provide a way of escape.

We must expect God to fight our battles.

God loves us and our families. We belong to Him. He is enough to keep our families in His hands and in His care.

Pray for the ones whom you love. Prayer is the only thing that changes people through God's love. God can change our hearts and minds through His Word and He is the only one who can make lasting change for the better, for and in our families. Each one of the members of our family can come to know the pure, morally correct love of our Father, Abba, and learn from that to understand how to love others.

This is the way that Generational curses are broken and new coping skills and ways of communicating and forgiving are learned. We can learn positive ways of moving forward with no losses!

THE TIME IS NOW! WE HAVE BEEN CHOSEN FOR THIS TASK! HANDLE IT GOD!

LEARNING CONTENTMENT IS KEY TO A PROPER RELATIONSHIP WITH YOUR HIGHER POWER

I t is imperative to live in contentment. Remember, it is by God's Grace and Mercy that we are forgiven. Remember that everyone struggles. Remember that some days are better than others. We do not earn our way to Heaven.

If you pride yourself on your own perfection, you are trying to steal the glory from God Almighty. Anytime you put down God's handiwork, you are claiming that your opinion is better than God's and that it should be valued as higher importance than God's.

The truth is of God's word says that "In my weakness, His strength shines." How we manage and deal with the hard times is what shows the real strength of a person and the God they serve.

The true power of a testimony is the test that they endured and the power of their God to change the heart of the person enduring. Strength is not found in how perfect you look, dress, live, dress or talk. Strength is found in who you rely on to be your provider of peace. If you look for a mortal man or woman, how easily can they be taken from you? True peace is knowing that God loves you unconditionally and will never leave you or forsake you. Even in our old age and gray hair He will sustain us. We must rely on Faith in Jesus to be the substance that we live on. He is before all things, He is in all things, and because Him all things exist.

If you give credit to perceived perfection, He sometimes gives you a thorn in your flesh so that you do not boast in your own power.

Remain humble and teachable. Shine His light. Embrace life. Challenge yourself to live by the Serenity prayer. God, grant me the serenity to accept the things I cannot change, the courage to change the things you can and the wisdom to know the difference.

The key is to pray and admit you are powerless over your life and give God control of your future. He has much better plans for us than we can imagine. He can do more in one minute of surrender and prayer than you can do in years of worry. He can teach you coping mechanisms through faith and the scriptures. He can teach you contentment through rest and peace. He can teach you motivation through directing your paths.

Sometimes when we examine our character defects and the scriptures and learn to forgive and surrender, He heals us from even our thorns in the flesh. The bible says that un-forgiveness can cause sickness. It even says that because of un-forgiveness we can be given over to the tormenters. That is serious! Remember, in Harry Potter – when the dementors came for someone? They determined that the best tactic against the dementors is a good 'memory' of any kind. In the Bible it says "If anything is good or pure, think on these things." Laugh, Love, Live and forgive.

Let's make a commitment to forgive. Let's make a commitment to work on ourselves. Let's make a commitment to live fully alive. Let's make a commitment to Love like we've never been hurt. Jesus died on the cross so that we can live victoriously through Him. Give his death value through your life that you choose to live.

But God. Everything will be ok in the end. If it is not ok, It is not the end.

I CLAIM THAT EVERYONE WHO HAS EVER BEEN GIVEN OVER TO THE TORMENTERS BECAUSE OF UNFORGIVENESS IS RELEASED BY POWER, LOVE AND A SOUND MIND. I PRAY THAT WE WILL BE MADE WHOLE BY GOD ALMIGHTY! I PRAY THAT OUR BODIES, SPIRITS, WILLS AND SOULS ARE COMPLETE IN HIM AND THAT WE ARE HEALED, WHOLE, STABLE AND MAINTAINED BY THE HOLY SPIRIT.

PERFECT PARENTS

There is no such thing as a perfect parent. We all make mistakes. Failure is only a temporary thing, life goes on.

We can all learn from each day we are given. When we know better, we do better.

To be here for our kids means making memories. Every-day, we are given opportunities to make cherished memories that last a lifetime. Take time to be present in the present!

Go get ice cream or donuts. Go to the park and feed the ducks or go fishing. Play a board game. Wrestle on the floor. Play hide and seek. Make homework fun! Cook a meal together, bake cookies.

BE THERE!

That's what It takes to be a good Mom, or Dad, Nana, Grandma or Grandad or Papa.

Be present in life, right now, right here, at this moment for the ones that you love! Cherish each moment!

WHOLENESS

Not everyone has your best interest. Be careful and learn discernment.

There have been times in my kid's lives that I had to get second opinions about the care they received.

When my daughter was born, the Doctor gave me pamphlets of institutions that he said that I should send her to. Expectancy for Down Syndrome kids was 25. I decided to keep her because I had begged God for a baby. She was just what I needed, and she needed me. Being a care giver made me a stronger person. I did it afraid until it became natural. I am not perfect, but God's strength shines in my weaknesses.

The skills that I learned were needed when my son was born as well. When he was 3 years old, he was tested for seizures. When the test came back, the Doctor's said that he showed activity like an adult seizure. They wanted me to put him on medication. For him to take the medication, I would have to sign a form saying that I would not sue if he became disabled or died as a result. I refused! They transferred him to another hospital, and we did a week-long EEG for children his age. The results came back normal. Doctors then said that it was a type of sleep apnea and that he would grow out of it. No medication needed.

When I had my stroke and became disabled, the Doctor's told me that I would never be able to work again and that my memory would never be good enough for me to even take classes. After my gastric bypass surgery, I lost 80 lbs, got off insulin, high blood pressure and high cholesterol meds and had more energy. I began to take classes in college. My first class was Anatomy and physiology. I made A's and B's.

However, when I tried to take nursing, I made a D. I might not be able to do it all, but I can do more than they expected. God's power can change us into His Story!

Since then, I have relied on discernment and Jesus to help us navigate.

I have learned that when Jesus is your source, The Source never runs out and He will supply all our needs according to His riches in Glory.

Health and healing are something that God has promised us in His word. He said that by Jesus stripes we are healed. Jesus died on the cross 2000 years ago and no further sacrifice is needed to heal us and make us whole! We are whole and complete in Christ!

Jesus is alive and well and the same spirit that raised Jesus from the dead lives in us and will raise Christians to life anytime this world gets overwhelming. Jesus can make sense out of chaos and still the storm. Jesus can give us His peace that passes all understanding.

There is now no condemnation in Christ. Jesus is the name above all names. It's not about religion, it's about the relationship.

The devil comes to divide and conquer, steal, kill and destroy. True Christians help the work of the body of Christ by unity and communion. Helping families to heal together united. Healed families create healed communities. Let's choose to let God be God and do His work in His timing and celebrate the things that we have in common and delight in the differences.

United we stand, divided we fall. Even in the fall, God forgives, loves, and encourages us back into wholeness in Christ.

What is my WHY?

What Hurts You?

What hurts me?

I have felt overwhelmed as a single Mom of typically developing kids and special needs kids. I have felt like there are no employment opportunities for me or my kids. I have felt like there are no resources available to handle the crisis that we face. I have felt like everyone is more interested in dividing us rather than supporting us. I have felt like I am in a fight to keep my identity.

I feel like people have used and abused single parents for far too long and gone through them sifting them as wheat. I feel that parents of special needs kids sometimes feel the struggle the most.

Jesus Christ came to identify with All of us! He has felt neglected, abused and used. This year we have all learned the value of ALL! Jesus died for ALL! Jesus loves ALL! This is the year we ask for Real Recovery with No Losses!

With Jesus, everyone can turn their mess into a message.

WHY?

What Helps You?

What Helps Me?

I stand on the scriptures: God's word says that if I commit my works to Him then He will establish my thoughts and the works of my hands.

I now have 3 jobs and work at places where I help teach inclusion and acceptance for ALL!

I have a list of resources that get State and Federal Funding to handle crisis of low-income families.

I have allowed God to multiply those of my family and friends into a Village or our own community that helps care for those we love.

I have found LegalShield to help represent me to keep my identity intact and guard my reputation online and monitor my information to keep it safe from the dark web for a small monthly fee that pays for itself with the benefits that come with my sanity and peace of mind.

I have found My Forever Family = Recovery for All of life's Hurts, Habits and Hangups!

My WHY became My Why when I admitted my powerlessness and surrendered to God.

Every-day is a new beginning and God's Grace is new each Morning!

Christ is in me and we live as Overcomers! God put me in Christ and I am a new creation! I have a Hope and a Future in Christ in me! No further sacrifices are needed because Jesus was the ultimate sacrifice 2000 years ago! Our sin debt is paid and we are forgiven and His!

He is All Powerful! We are powerless, but we can never lose anything that we put in God's hands!

kellysimpson9.wearelegalshield.com

RECOVERY

SURRENDERING TO GOD AND REALIZING THAT HE IS A SPIRITUAL BEING THAT WILL NEVER LEAVE YOU OR FORSAKE YOU

SETTING AND OWNING YOUR BOUNDARIES

GET UP, DRESS UP AND SHOW UP, GOD WILL DO THE REST

POSSESS YOUR POSSESSIONS, TAKE OWNERSHIP OF YOUR ATTITUDE

WORK, PAY YOUR BILLS, HANDLE YOUR BUSINESS!

HAVE NO EXPECTATIONS FROM ANYONE OTHER THAN GOD, HUMANS CAN DISAPPOINT YOU, GOD NEVER WILL

ALWAYS COMMUNICATE, PAUSE WHEN AGITATED, PRAY WHEN YOU PAUSE

FORGIVE YOURSELF AND IF YOU AND GOD HAVE DEALT WITH YOUR SIN AND YOUR PAST, DON'T LET ANYONE ELSE BRING IT UP!

*TRUST GOD AND LOVE PEOPLE

LIVE AND LET LIVE

SMILE, REST, RECUPERATE

ALWAYS GET BACK UP AND TRY AGAIN

NEVER GIVE UP

INSPIRE, ENCOURAGE, REMEMBER THAT EVERYONE STRUGGLES

EVEN IF GOD IS THE ONLY ONE YOU SHARE YOUR BURDENS WITH. LEARN TO SHARE YOUR PAIN "A BURDEN SHARED IS HALF A BURDEN"

KEEP THE FAITH. KEEP LOOKING UP. REMEMBER HOW FAR YOU'VE COME

YOU CAN NEVER LOSE ANYTHING THAT IS IN GOD'S HANDS

RECOVERY CAN BE FROM MANY THINGS

HEALTH, RELATIONSHIPS, SUBSTANCE ABUSE, PEOPLE, OVEREATING, CONTROL ISSUES

TRAUMA AND HURT IS THE BEGINNING BUT HEALING AND JESUS CAN BE THE NEW OUTCOME

HE HEALS, HE RESTORES, HE RENEWS, HE RECOVERS. HE ESTABLISHES!

NOTHING IS WASTED!

WE ARE FORGIVEN, WE ARE WHOLE, WE ARE CHOSEN, WE ARE LOVED

WALK IN YOUR FREEDOM. POSSESS YOUR POSSESSIONS. RECLAIM YOUR LIFE

OWN YOUR LIFE

IN OUR WEAKNESS, HIS STRENGTH SHINES!

WORLD CELEBRATION DAYS

March 21st is World Down Syndrome Day! That's the day the world celebrates Down Syndrome!

My daughter has Down Syndrome. She is 30 years old. I cherish every moment with her.

The world has made tremendous strides in achieving awareness and advancement in the lives of those with Down Syndrome. Even since my daughter's birth. Years ago, most individuals with Down Syndrome only lived around 25 years and they were sometimes institutionalized and kept away from their families.

My daughter graduated High School and went on to be a teacher assistant at a daycare. She taught kids colors, numbers, letters and the days of the weeks and months of the year. She now has a full-time job doing what she loves. She has a roommate and pays her own bills.

October 1st is World ADHD Day!

My son had ADHD when he was younger. I treasure my

time with him. Since his childhood, he has outgrown ADHD and he has learned valuable coping skills. He also has a job and a family that he loves.

My grandkids are precious, and I dearly love them!

Having my children has taught me empathy and understanding for all kinds. Love and acceptance can truly change people's lives for the better.

Friends celebrate the differences and delight in the things that they have in common.

I now work as a Caseworker at a preschool. Here in my profession, we work with all families. Some struggle with disabilities, mental health, and all of life's challenges.

My experiences, strengths and hope are applied and practiced every day to remind others to push through and grow into all that we can be and to rely on each other for support.

Never stop! Never give up! Overcome! Challenge Life!

Leave a legacy of love and acceptance!

Be present in the present!

One thing that I am sure of is that God is God. He is in control. I have seen time after time, accusations against God's people come to naught. God sees all! God knows all! God balances the scales! People think that because someone has a past it is easy to blame them for all their problems and they think that they will get away with it. That is not the case. Keep your head up. Stay in the scriptures. You are the righteousness in Christ Jesus. The spirit and the seed of God live in you. There is no darkness in Him and therefore there is no darkness in you. He will fight your battles. You must pray and do his will.

Jesus is my husband, my provider, my redeemer, my vindicator, my health, my strength, my everything. If you do what He asked you to do He will handle what you ask Him to do. Pray without ceasing. God's got us! We are His!

You must not live by people's compliments, if you do, you will die by their criticisms. Try not to speak your own words to fight your battles. Find a scripture, use God's words. Impact the Spiritual Realm. Change your destiny. Prophecy your future. Speak forth things as you wish them to be until they are.

I have the mind of Christ. I am a productive member of society. My vehicles are covered by the blood of Jesus and no further sacrifice is needed other than the death of Jesus on the cross 2 thousand years ago.

I have healthy relationships with my family. I have proper boundaries and God grants me wisdom when people try to take advantage of me on how to handle it without being overcome with un-forgiveness and offense. God is my vindicator. He is who I get my rewards from, because of this, I do not have unmet expectations from people in my life.

He is my peace, He is my comfort, He is my future and my Hope.

Statistics

Many of you have heard God's call, you know you have a purpose to do great things for God. Many of us pray for God to open doors for us to be missionaries or preachers or evangelists to foreign countries. I am here to tell you that God has called you. He does not call the qualified, he qualifies the called. You don't have to wait, God has placed you in your mission field right where you are this very day. Bloom where you are planted and God will reveal your harvest. Look around you in this room. Here are some statistics I have found about people in our everyday life.

A. Fatherlessness
1. 27 million (39% of kids under age 18) live in a home without a dad. Approximately half of these kids haven't seen their dad in the last year.

2. 25% of kids who live in homes with a dad spend less than one hour a day with their dad.

B. Sexual Abuse
1. As many as 1 out of 4 children are sexually abused by someone they love or should be able to trust.
2. Many survivors of sexual abuse have never talked about it to anyone.

C. Sexual Addiction
1. In a congregation of 500 people, as many as 50 will struggle with sexual addiction or addiction to pornography.
2. The internet has increased accessibility to pornography and FALSE INTIMACY.

D. Depression
1. 20% of Americans will, at some time during their life, experience clinical depression.
2. Women tend to experience depression 2 times more frequently than men.

E. Anxiety
1. 1 out of 6 people experiences some type of debilitating anxiety.
2. Panic Attacks and Obsessive- Compulsive Disorder are just 2 examples of the anxiety controlling people's lives.

F. Stress
1. "Hurried Sickness" The persistent belief that there's never enough time.

2. The result of stress escalation - crowded lives + fatigue + insensitivity + irritability = Isolation and Loneliness.

3. Stress affects us physically causing heart attacks, high blood pressure, etc.

G. Marital Conflicts

1. At least 50% who marry today will divorce.

2. These statistics don't include the sorrow that occurs "behind closed doors."

H. Childhood Struggles

1. "latchkey kids" - a generation of lonely children.

2. Approximately 18 million kids today are in need of some type of therapeutic intervention.

I. Struggling Adolescents

1. They search for identity and acceptance.

2. Approximately 1 million teenage girls will end up pregnant each year. Nearly ½ will have abortions.

3. Drug and alcohol dependency are high. People try to cope by trying to fill the sense of emptiness by seeking medications or try to self-medicate by taking street drugs.

4. Teens sometimes lack clear direction, goals and commitment because they have not been taught it.

5. Suicide has become the #2 killer of our teens.

2 Corinthians 5:18 says "But all things are of God, who reconciled us to himself through Christ, and gave us the ministry of reconciliation."

Galatians 6:1 "Brethren, even if a man be overtaken in any trespass, ye who are spiritual, restore such one in a spirit of gentleness; looking to thyself, lest thou also be tempted."

Ephesians 4:11-12 '& he gave some to be apostles; & some prophets; & some pastors and teachers. For the perfecting of the saints, unto the work of ministering, unto the building up of the body of Christ."

James 5:15 "& The prayer of faith shall save him that is sick, & the Lord shall raise him up; and if he have committed sins, it shall be forgiven him.

This is your mission field, the future belongs to those that show up!

Everyone we meet every day is going through their own personal battle. We have the power to crush their spirit or encourage them in their journey. Start yours today in your mission field.

God's power is not intimidated by your circumstances. You're empowered by God to reach & accomplish goals that transcend human limitations.

www.aacc.net

You're Enough!

I woke up one morning and told God that I need Him every second of every day. I need Him to live in me and fill me with His Holy Spirit. I need Him to help me breathe, start my day and even to do the small daily tasks.

I told Him that the only voice that I want to hear is His. I want Him to be the still small voice that I hear. Since then, the things that I heard spoken over me went from "You're stupid or you're a nut" went to "I'm so proud of you and You're Enough."

I've totally changed the people, places and things that I surround myself with. I call people for prayer, I have prayer partners. I pray with my coworkers. I pray with my church members. I pray for my city and nation. I pray for all of those in my circle of influence. I pray for my family, all of them.

When I get to Heaven, I want Jesus to say well done, my good and faithful servant for all the ones that you brought to me.

Every second is to be treasured and each day is a gift! Give it to God and He will supply all of our needs according to His riches in Glory. He will fight our battles. He is before all things and in Him, all things hold together. Colossians 1:17.

Empowering Families

"Much can be done when we raise our voices and join together. We cannot simply stand by and wait for someone else to take action. We must make our own history!" Ken Ervin

What is self determination – an idea that includes people choosing and setting their own goals, being involved in making decisions, self advocating and working to reach their goals. It is not about control! It is about taking action in your life to get the things that you want and need. It usually contributes to positive results in areas like employment, education, community living and improved quality of life. (Wehmeyer et al. 2003)

. . .

Community Advocacy – a preventative approach that enables people to be active citizens and self advocate in regards to decisions affecting their lives.

My question to myself was – what do I want to do? My answer is simple:

I want to empower families, including mine, to handle the challenges that we face in today's world.

To do this, there are some topics of concern that came to mind: Reducing fatherlessness, encouraging co-parenting, single parenting, child support, help for incarcerated parents, reducing child poverty, encouraging work, family support from the community as a whole, and opportunities for leadership development for all.

Communities must know what resources and supports are available to help in all areas.

In doing research, I found that In the mid 60'S, during the War on Poverty, Project Head Start was created. The Johnson Administration was determined "to eliminate the paradox of poverty in the nation by opening to everyone to live in decency and dignity." (Norton et al. 1986)

I am currently working at a Head Start program. I want to further pursue my career by instilling the following goals for myself, my family and others. I want to work at a job that I am passionate about and that I can give my everything and have it nurtured, multiplied and where we will be equipped and prepared to provide stability for my family and others in the community.

I would like to build bridges in our community that bring about change for the better with no losses. Fault finding is a thing of the past and encouragement, support and guidance is the proper path for the future.

Malachi 4:6 Challenge is to Turn hearts back to God, Family and kingdom values.

This goal can be accomplished by: Empowering families to be strong, productive members of society. This is key to sustainability for communities as a whole.

I would like to help to-

-Provide support and mentoring services and facilitate local level communication and coordination between Head Start and other agencies in our community.

- Increase the participation of parents and other significant people in the lives of kids.

-Development of intervention and prevention programs in the community.

-Provide sessions to alleviate some of the stereotypical views toward males, those with disabilities and collaboration between parents.

-Provide intensive training in parenting.

- Provide information on literacy training classes, medical, dental, legal, psychological counseling, recovery when needed.

- Provide avenues for each person to be active citizens in their community and opportunities for leadership and involvement.

-Reiterate that you don't have to be a perfect parent or a perfect person to be present in the present.

9 = MINISTRY

Each of us are chosen in our own way by God who is the author of our unique story. Only He is the author and finisher of our Faith! Each obstacle that each of us have endured is the very thing that God has called us to be in Ministry for. That is the very thing that has prepared and equipped us for that particular ministry.

Just like there is no perfect parents, there are no perfect people in Ministry either. Only Jesus is perfect. We can strive to always do the right thing, but when we fall, we must always look to Jesus for forgiveness and restoration. He can and He will with encouragement, strength and hope.

Morning Devotions this morning said Hebrews 8:12 I will be merciful to their unrighteousness, and their sins... I will remember no more. "God makes a remarkable promise to us. He doesn't just forgive us. He forgets that we've ever sinned. He erases the board. He destroys the evidence. He burns the microfilm. He clears the computer. He doesn't remember our mistakes. For all the things He does do, this is one thing he refuses to do. He refuses to keep a list of all my wrongs."

He forgives so we can too! We can forgive others and love others and let God clean them and restore peace to our lives in proper relationships with meaningful conversations. We can rely on Him to help us have and maintain proper boundaries with those in our presence. He gives us a Power, Love and a Sound Mind and the ability and fruits of the Spirit to overcome respectfully to all that we encounter.

Exodus 14:14 says The Lord will fight for you; you need only be still. Stick and Stay. Bloom where you're planted. Shine in the storm. Shine Jesus' light through all your words, actions and deeds. SPARKLE!

I am part of several ministries now and I'm enjoying it. I volunteer in the nursery. I work as a caseworker. I'm a house Mom for an unwed pregnant women's home. I'm a Mother to my children and a grandmother to my grandkids. I volunteer with Aglow. I am a friend to those that God has given me and to the ones that He chose to be in my life. God gives me the privilege of ministering to all of the above the best way I know how.

You don't have to have a college education. You don't have to like people. You don't have to be perfect. If God lays it on your heart to serve Him. DO IT! Get up, Dress up and Show up! He will provide the opportunity! The anointing is not about being the gift. It is about serving. Jesus is worthy of our service.

When we serve others, God creates positions for opportunities. God's word says: Psalm 90:17 And let the beauty of the

Lord our God be upon us: and establish thou the work of our hands.

Don't die without first LIVING!

When you hear my story, I want you to see God in His infinite wisdom changing my life for His good, working on my behalf, being my intercessor, and making my mess into His story. My story is His, I'm just the one telling it.

9 years ago, I was enslaved by fear and torment, nightmares and living Hell on earth!

I knew that I needed God to make changes in my life because I had tried and failed miserably. I finally let and let God. I did the next right thing. I went to several churches and made friends who would ride out even the bad days. I got phone numbers and lost the fear not to call anyone for help.

I started going to recovery groups and fully relying on God to change me. I always remembered that My God sent mate and friends will never pull me away from my family or my God given assignments.

I learned what true freedom is and settled down in a job. I have now been employed for 8 years and God has allowed me to buy a house and a car of my own. I started off as a substitute teacher and then I got promoted to Caseworker and now I'm in classes to be a Center Coordinator. But God!

I'm reminded again, that God knows my future and He's already there.

I have been abused, neglected and sometimes left for dead, but the same spirit that raised Jesus from the dead lives in me and will raise me up every time! If God will do this for me, imagine what He'll do for you!

It is only by the Grace of God that I'm alive and well. I thank Him for every breath I breathe. Thanks for being my forever family!